Lamplight Collection of Modern Art

Matisse and the Fauves

by RENATA NEGRI

Lamplight Publishing, Inc.
New York, New York

PUBLISHED IN THE UNITED STATES OF AMERICA IN 1975
by Lamplight Publishing, Inc., N.Y. 10016

First published in the series "Mensili d'Arte" Copyright © 1967
by Fratelli Fabbri Editori, Milan, Italy

Illustrations Copyright © 1970 by Fratelli Fabbri Editori, Milan,
Italy on the American Edition.

ALL RIGHTS RESERVED, PRINTED IN ITALY

Library of Congress Catalog Card Number: 70-1066-57

SBN 0-88308-013-3

The Birth of Fauvism

It was Louis Vauxcelles, the Parisian art critic, who christened the first true revolution in twentieth-century art. During a visit to the famous Salon d'Automne in 1905, Vauxcelles noticed a classic Florentine bronze lost and overwhelmed among the richly colorful and flamboyantly nontraditional paintings of Matisse, Vlaminck, Marquet, and Derain. The shocked critic exclaimed derisively: *"Donatello parmi les fauves"* (a Donatello caged among wild beasts). Vauxcelles' witticism was printed that very evening as part of a newspaper review of the Salon. From that day on, the small group of artists at whom Vauxcelles aimed his barbed criticism became known as the *Fauves* (wild beasts) and were considered to be part of a new movement in art, Fauvism. But if Fauvism was, as art historians say, a violent revolution, it was fought to free artists from all prior restraints—rules, conventions, traditions—that limited their free use of color.

Fauvism was born in a casual, improvised fashion. There were no manifestos or doctrines that spelled out a Fauvist credo. Instead, it was actually a meeting in time of exceptional individuals who, at a given point in their creative development, found similar means of breaking away from academic convention. This very casualness and lack of central doctrine may explain the brief life of Fauvism (1905–1907) and why its members later took completely different roads—from Matisse's love affair with the sun to the stupendous lyricism in Braque's rational lines; from Dufy's decorative and poetic caligraphy to Vlaminck's dramatic violence; from Van Dongen's worldliness to Derain's noble classicism. Yet, in spite of a lack of internal cohesiveness, Fauvism was a movement of extreme importance. Although Fauvism had few adherents and was to last as a movement for a few years only, it had a tremendously liberating effect on art as it moved out of the nineteenth century and into the twentieth. In its dedication to brilliant color and its imperious disregard of perspective and freedom to alter spacial relationships, Fauvist art was a giant step toward freeing the creative imagination from any obligation to imitate nature.

Its Origins and Components

More than anything else, Fauvism is an expression of the joyful, vital explosion of feeling by young artists in love with the world and anxious to express their love through color. The strength of Fauvism lay in its desire to break away from all preceding experiences. However, preceding traditions and movements in art cannot be suddenly obliterated. And as with all other revolutions, Fauvism had its roots in the artistic phenomena that came before it and was deeply indebted to the great personalities that appeared on the artistic scene at the turn of the century. It would be natural to ask whether the Fauves would have found the same means of expression without the tradition-breaking discoveries of Seurat, Cézanne, Van Gogh, or Gauguin. But even an acknowledged debt to others could never diminish the merits of Matisse and his colleagues. They knew how to profit from the best features at the turn of the century and, at the same time, how to create a new artistic language for their particular goals.

Although it may seem strange today, now that time has given the proper perspective to the extraordinary artistic season as the nineteenth century drew to a close, the artists most sought after at the beginning of the twentieth century by museums and galleries were not Cézanne, Gauguin, or Van Gogh but the now nearly forgotten traditionalists and Academicians who exhibited their works in the official salons. They were the ones whose paintings sold for high prices and who received favorable reviews in the papers. Cézanne, Seurat, Van Gogh, and Gauguin, the painters whom we value so highly today, were on the other hand practically unknown to the public, even if they were admired by some dealers and critics. As the twentieth century opened, the Impressionist painters were still looked upon with mistrust. Even as late as 1894, the Louvre contemptuously rejected a group of Impressionist works. This clearly demonstrated the gap between the popular taste of the times that mirrored the values of a bourgeois society afraid of innovation and the avant-garde painters who were desperately seeking new means of expression. While this bourgeois society was still perplexed by the works of Monet and Renoir, gifted young artists such as Matisse and his colleagues considered Impressionism an established art form that they had already gone beyond. This continual movement toward new means of expression was a logical consequence of the artistic strides made in the last twenty years of the nineteenth century that produced all the precursors of the art of our times.

In those twenty years alone, both Rousseau's lyrical primitivism and Cézanne's revolutionary vision had found a place in the world of art. Van Gogh's correlation between feeling and color and his desire to extract symbols from reality and to find a hitherto unreachable truth in the natural world were also a part of those extraordinary times. And along with the art of the Symbolists — the Pont-Aven group, Redon, and the Nabis painters — we find Seurat's Pointillism, which was based on scientific research and aimed at establishing the autonomy of the painting as an expression of a truth that no longer mirrored the momentary and volatile reality of the Impressionists but rather sought absolute and independent values. All these artists and movements contributed to the formation of the Fauves and became a stimulus and an indispensable tool for their artistic expression. In fact, the Fauves went through a Pointillist stage, were influenced by Van Gogh, learned about internal order and balance of the canvas from Cézanne, imitated Gauguin's fabulous *aplat* in order to create more brilliant tableaus, and still managed to create something completely new and different. The Fauvist idea that a painting is the expression of a harmonious reality governed by a perfect internal balance is not far removed from the visions of Cézanne and Seurat.

The Role of Matisse

The Fauves were indebted to Van Gogh and Gauguin not only for the means they used to achieve balance but also for the obvious two-dimensional planes, the dominant role of color, and their emphasis on primary colors spread *aplat* or captured in flaming brushstrokes. Yet Fauvism was born in a climate of dissent against the past and sought even greater freedom of expression. Therefore the Fauves rejected Seurat's intellectual preoccupations, Van Gogh's sentimental components, and Gauguin's overly symbolistic allusions. Pure painting originated with the Fauves, especially with Matisse. This art reflects an existential happiness subject only to instinctive nonscientific laws of color harmony. Such a simple and yet so efficient a formulation could stem only from an exceptional artistic personality. Thus it was Matisse who is usually recognized as the leader of the movement because he gave it a cohesiveness that could not other-

Matisse *Piano Lesson*, 1916 (245.1 x 213.4 cm)
New York, Museum of Modern Art

Matisse *Goldfish and Sculpture*, 1911 (116.8 x 100.6 cm)
New York, Museum of Modern Art

wise have existed. Naturally the art and concepts of Matisse are not all there is to Fauvism; such artists as André Derain and Maurice Vlaminck prove this, but without Henri Matisse, Fauvism could not have existed.

In the first years of our century there was a great need to start art anew by exploring all the possibilities of expression through color. The chromatic violence of the Brücke (Bridge) group's first experiments and the early flaming canvases of Kandinsky and Jawlensky are excellent examples. Matisse's paintings were the result of this tendency, which assumed great importance among French artists during that period. In 1896 Valtat was already using brilliant color in luminous combinations in much the same way that Matisse and the Fauves were to use it in later years. Toward the beginning of the twentieth century Kees van Dongen, the Dutch artist, followed an altogether personal road but later moved toward the principles of Fauvism. Vlaminck was the first artist to use a completely Fauvist idiom in his landscapes of 1903 and 1904. Nevertheless it was only through Matisse's lucid insights that Fauvism acquired its own character and reached full maturity.

Henri Matisse was born into a middle-class family in 1869 in Le Cateau, France. In 1892, while recovering from an attack of appendicitis during his law studies, Matisse took up painting to pass time and liked it so much that, in spite of his father's objections, he decided to give up the law and go to Paris to take painting lessons. Thus, at the age of twenty-two, Matisse began his first formal study of art in the studio of Guillaume Bouguereau, a leading Academician. But Bouguereau's formalism was not agreeable to Matisse, who soon moved to the atelier of the artistically liberal Gustave Moreau. Rouault, Piot, Evenepoel, Camoin, Manguin, and Marquet, all future Fauves, were also Moreau's students at this time. Matisse had previously met Marquet, and from then on the two became inseparable and devoted friends.

Encouraged by Moreau, who recognized his great artistic gifts, Matisse dedicated himself to the improvement of his technique and alternated his exercises at the atelier with frequent visits to the Louvre, where he carefully studied and copied the classic masterpieces.

Matisse visited Belle-Île in 1896 and 1897, and there his canvas began to show hints of the vivid, pure color that was to characterize his mature work. But it was in Corsica and Toulouse that the artist was first conquered by the blinding Mediterranean light. The thick yellow and red brushstrokes in his *Toulouse Landscape* (1898, Plate 1) reflect the warmth of the Mediterranean sunlight. In this painting there are evidences of both Impressionist and Pointillist influences that show Matisse's great drive to free his use of color from tradition once and for all. Other paintings of the same period that reveal Matisse's struggle to make color alone do all the work are his *Nude Study in the Atelier*, where the small, separate brushstrokes in the Pointillist style are used to obtain a maximum luminosity on the canvas. *Still Life* and *The Invalid* (Plate 2), which he completed in 1899, reveal a certain affinity with the Nabis but show greater chromatic virtuosity. Matisse's audacious use of color contrasts in this first period of his artistic life culminates in the *Interior with Harmonium* (1900, Plate 3).

By 1900, Matisse had obviously discovered the power of color but still did not know how to control it completely to achieve his goals or liberate it from natural forms and hues. Matisse, to whom Moreau had prophetically said "You will simplify painting," was now searching for essentials, for simpler means to greater results. In order to achieve his goals, he studied avidly and became quite interested in sculpture. Cézanne's painting, *The Bathers*, which Matisse bought in 1899 despite economic difficulties, was a determining factor in his career. From the art of Cézanne he learned that color can create space and volume and that shades of color are forces that must find their right balance within the painting. From 1901 to 1903, Matisse had serious financial difficulties and went through a period of retreat and meditation. During this time he produced few paintings and these in rather dull colors.

The First: Marquet

In this dark period of Matisse's life his faithful friend Marquet was always nearby. Marquet was the most singular of the Fauves because of the frank contrast between his shy personality that led him to paint in a subtle, delicate style and Fauvism's violent expression. However, the firmness of Marquet's design and the elegance of his lines, even in his early years, were significant contributions to the making of Fauvism. During the time when both were students at Moreau's atelier, Marquet, like Matisse, used unusually brilliant blues and oranges. In his youthful boldness (he was only twenty-three years old in 1898), Marquet followed Matisse in his most adventurous experiments with colors. His *Life Class at the École des Beaux-Arts* (Plate 4), similar in style to Matisse's Pointillist paintings, confirmed Marquet's exceptional potential even at that time. In this painting the feminine body, which Matisse taught him to love and interpret as a simple and perfect piece of architecture, acquires a singular plasticity. The background is a celebration of dots of color, a free interpretation of the Pointillist technique that imparts a gleam to the entire canvas. Marquet's gifted use of color is manifested in a more mature fashion in a painting done in

1903, *Nude at the Atelier of a Friend,* in which vermilion against green and nocturnal blues is treated with remarkable firmness.

After Moreau's death in 1898, Matisse attended the Académie Camillo, where he met other young artists who were attracted by his zeal and extraordinary personality. Besides Marquet, Manguin, Camoin, and Linaret, who had already met him while he studied under Moreau, Matisse was now associated with an ever-widening circle of young students including Carrière, Puy, Chabaud, Laprade, and, most important, André Derain.

The Two from Chatou

Derain was to play a very special role in the Fauve group. Aside from his personal contribution as a great protagonist of the Fauvist ideal and as a catalyst, he also served to bring together the two strongest and most different personalities of the movement: Henri Matisse and Maurice Vlaminck. Matisse, strongly influenced by the art of Europe, the near East, and the Orient, and in search of an ideal of peace and beauty, would appear to have been in direct opposition to Vlaminck's savage and vehement rejection of all that had gone before. Indeed, Vlaminck bragged about not knowing the museums and maintained that he wanted to ignore everything that had ever happened in the world of art in order to paint only as his heart dictated.

Matisse and Vlaminck met through Derain in 1901 at a retrospective exhibit of Van Gogh's paintings. Vlaminck's feverish reaction ("That day I loved Van Gogh more than my father," he said) was typical of his impassioned approach to life and art. Matisse quickly recognized Vlaminck's merits as an artist, and a year later Derain invited Matisse to visit him and Vlaminck at their studio in Chatou. The older artist was impressed by the work he saw and invited Derain and Matisse to show their paintings with his group in the Salon des Indépendants of 1903.

André Derain was born in 1880 in the country village of Chatou, France, and grew up there. He had a restless spirit and loved experimentation and research. Although his merchant family tried to hamper his career, their efforts were in vain. At the early age of fifteen his painting showed great promise, and at the age of eighteen he had already completed his art studies at the Académie Carrière in Paris, where he spent much of his time practicing by copying classical paintings. Maurice de Vlaminck, who was born in Paris in 1876, had a strong athlete's body and a great natural talent for music. In his youth Vlaminck earned his living bicycle racing and playing the violin in Paris nightclubs. He had a kind of physical vitality that is rare to find in the art world; he did not merely approach the canvas—he assailed it and mixed and twirled the colors until he became dizzy from them.

In 1899 Vlaminck left Paris and moved to the country near Chatou. Shortly afterward he met Derain on a train, and the two liked each other so well that they decided to work together from the next day on. As the Impressionists had done, they placed their easels side by side and painted in the open air.

Derain, who was much more introspective and complicated than Vlaminck, labored arduously to find his way. *The Bedroom,* painted in 1900, showed Matisse's influence in the reds and blues of the table as well as in the rhythm of the structural plains that resemble *Interior with Harmonium.* Vlaminck, in contrast, faced the canvas without any conflicts, and in 1900 he painted *At the Bar* (Plate 8), which is daring both for its composition and for its violent use of color. His discovery of Van Gogh was the spark that ignited his stormy, artistic personality.

While Derain was away from Chatou fulfilling his military service from 1901 to 1904, and Matisse was going through a period of financial problems and introspection and had put aside pure colors, Vlaminck was alone in Chatou reflecting on Van Gogh's works. During this period, in 1903, he produced paintings such as *The Pond at Saint-Cucufa* (Plate 9), which is a lyrical landscape of woods and waters, where the reds, greens, and browns sway in unison under a blue sky. In 1904, while his colors became hotter and more violent, he went from the intense emerald green and purple of *Kitchen Interior* (Plate 10) to the segmented rhythm of *Houses at Chatou* (Plate 11), in which Van Gogh's influence is most vivid. It was at that point that Vlaminck assumed the role of momentary leader of the Fauves. His great artistic convictions and his passionate nature let him overcome all the theoretical and conceptual difficulties that had troubled and inhibited other artists in the movement.

Vlaminck's art was like his life, rebellious and unconventional. He applied his paints directly from the tube and looked at nature only to forget it and paint the images mirrored in his own ardent and passionate soul.

Derain, who matured considerably during his three years of military service, went through a personal crisis deciding between Matisse and Vlaminck's diametrically opposed positions. He was tortured by impossible choices between passion and contemplation, between culture and instinct. Finally, in 1904, Derain was able to finish his first paintings in a truly Fauvist style. Among them were his bright *Barges* (Plate 12), as well as *The Old Tree* (Plate 13), a painting filled with marvelous chromatic effects of green and violet.

Around the Protagonists

For many of the Fauves 1904 was a decisive year. Puy did paintings in which color is wonderfully controlled within a framework that oscillates between Cézanne's art and Gauguin's love for "synthesis." Camoin's style matured during his military service in Aix, where he met Cézanne. His spontaneous and yet highly structured style can be clearly seen in his portrait of Marquet (Plate 17), as well as in his landscapes *The Port of Marseilles* (Plate 21) and *Moulin Rouge.*

Henri Manguin was one of the most daring artists of the group, for he was encouraged by his middle-class family to follow his artistic inclinations freely. Influenced by Matisse and Marquet, he evolved from a kind of art that was concerned with the simplifications of forms and the use of pure arbitrary color. This is clearly seen in his *Woman at the Window, Rue Boursault* (Plate 18), completed in 1904. The window frames the model and forms shadows around her, creating a splendid chromatic tension similar to Marquet's *Nude at the Atelier of a Friend.*

Kees van Dongen, who came to Paris from Holland in 1897, was slowly developing a very personal style. Like his countryman Van Gogh, he too emphasized the importance of color contrast in his painting. Van Dongen turned to the bistros for inspiration. In the fall of 1904 he exhibited his paintings with the Fauves for the first time at the Salon des Indépendants, where Matisse and Marquet had exhibited since 1901, followed by Manguin in 1902, and by Camoin, Puy, Dufy, and Friesz in 1903. Van Dongen's work reached maturity in 1905, simultaneously with Matisse and the most important artists in the group.

The year 1904 also marked a turning point for Matisse's art. It was then that he overcame his doubts with regard to painting and was finally able to master the use of color to his own satisfaction. He came upon this realization while spending the summer in Saint-Tropez on the Mediterranean Riviera with the Neo-Impressionist Paul Signac. The warm, bright beauty of the Mediterranean coast backed by its lush countryside contributed to Matisse's artistic evolution and stimulated him to find a means of expressing beauty and harmony both in the use of color and in the perfect balance of composition. Under the influence of Signac's Pointillist technique, Matisse filled his canvases with light and sparkling nuances that liberated him from the thick brushstrokes of his earlier paintings and allowed him to create more dramatic contrasts. Matisse, however, identified perfection with simplicity and rejected the Pointillists' scientific theories on optical effects and complementary colors. He adopted a Pointillist-like approach only out of a kind of artistic sensibility—as a means to a self-determined end.

Luxe, calme et volupté

This period of Matisse's career was marked by a painting that became a landmark for modern art: *Luxe, calme et volupté* (Plate 7), which Matisse finished in 1905 and exhibited at the Salon des Indépendants that spring. The bathers in this painting are both reality and myth; the reality becomes timeless through the artist's imaginative lyricism. The young girls are like nymphs in an enchanted garden; the sinuous lines that encircle the beach and the firm counterpoint of the vertical tree to the right create a perfect decorative balance. This painting perfectly expresses the Fauvist theory of doing away with ornamentation in order to achieve an essential truth of balance and harmony.

The Three from Le Havre

Luxe, calme et volupté was also a turning point for another young gifted artist, Raoul Dufy. His words in response to this painting became famous: "Looking at the painting I have understood the importance of renewal in art. Impressionistic realism has lost its fascination for me upon contemplating the miracle of imagination introduced in the form and colors of this painting." Dufy was twenty-three years old when he came to Paris in 1900 from Le Havre, where he had received an excellent art education. Othon Friesz and Georges Braque had been students at the same school with Dufy, and together they formed what came to be known as "the trio from Le Havre." These three, along with the two from Chatou, Matisse and Van Dongen, are the creators of the vivid, emotional, and often violent style that Vauxcelles was to label as Fauvism.

There were other artists whose works were occasionally reminiscent of Fauvism. We see hints of Fauvist-like expression in the paintings of Rouault, in spite of his dramatic expressionism, and in the early paintings of Kandinsky and Jawlensky. Other minor artists such as Chabaud and Marinot also became partially associated with the Fauves, but their excursions into Fauvism were more out of novelty than out of true belief in the theories of the movement. Dufy's attachment to Fauvism, on the other hand, was genuine and complete. Like Friesz and Braque, he had attempted an Impressionist style when he first moved to Paris, but it never satisfied him completely. It was Matisse's paintings that led Dufy to a meaningful expression of his art. For him too the problem was to crystalize emotion through the use of color and the simplicity of line. In 1905, after he discovered how ineffectual realistic Impressionism was for his purposes, his canvas was transformed. It was at that time that he painted *Old Houses on the Harbor of Honfleur* (Plate 24) and *Parasols* (Plate 25).

Matisse and Derain at Collioure

Friesz and Braque became associated with the Fauves only in 1906 while the rest of the group reached its apogee under Matisse's influence. In the summer of 1905, while Manguin, Marquet, and Camoin, following Matisse's footsteps, went to Saint-Tropez and painted some of their best works, Matisse went to Collioure (near Barcelona, Spain) with Derain. It was actually in that small Catalonian port that Fauvism reached its highest peak. In the spring of 1905 Matisse had organized retrospective collections of Seurat's and Van Gogh's works at the Salon des Indépendants. These retrospective shows were precious lessons for Matisse and guided his way, giving him the necessary peace of mind to abandon himself freely to his own inspiration in Collioure.

His stay in Collioure also brought Matisse in contact with some of Gauguin's last works, as well as with Daniel de Monfried, who lived there and who introduced Matisse and Derain to the sculptor Aristide Maillol. It was the right time and the right place for Matisse to liberate himself from the Pointillist influence. Gauguin's bright canvases, with their sensuous chromatic sweeps, showed Matisse the simplest way of arriving at pure colors and precise rhythmic compositions — at last he felt in complete control of his art.

The works Matisse painted during that fortunate summer in Spain were followed by even more important paintings. *Interior at Collioure* (Plate 28), *Open Window at Collioure*, Derain's portrait, *Pastoral* (Plate 27) are only precursors of the painting that became the symbol of Fauvism, *Study for "The Joy of Life"* (Plate 30). Leymarie commented: "This painting is an extraordinary synthesis of two themes that are traditionally opposites, the bachanal and the pastoral with the frenetic whirl of the dancers in the middle and the Arcadian softness of the nymphs and the shepherds in the foreground. Here it exalts Dionysius. there an Olympian peace. here the rhythm and there the melody. ...Matisse, in fact, surpasses the traditional contrast that separates Ingres from Delacroix, that which assigns the intellectual power to the lines and the passionate role to color. He considers art to be a mimesis [a mimic] of both the outer and the inner world, and finally attains the beatific, abstract Eastern concepts to which Mallarmé also aspired."

For Derain as well as for Matisse those months at Collioure brought about a decisive maturation that can be seen not only in the works he created there but also in the letters he wrote to Vlaminck. From this correspondence we learn how intelligently and with how much zeal Derain assimilated Matisse's lessons and how much he let himself be guided by the violent sensations that the scenery produced in him. His canvas now took on the splendor of the rainbow from cobalt blue and amethyst to chromatic yellows and pure reds. He dealt with the human figure in the same way he dealt with the landscape — his portrait of Matisse is a masterpiece expressed in an extremely daring and synthetic language — in freedom of color and design.

The custom of painting portraits of each other was a common pastime among the Fauves from the very beginning of the movement. The two portraits painted in Collioure are patent examples of the interest that the Fauves always had for the human figure, an interest similar to that which they had for scenery, even if less well known. Matisse himself said that nothing like the human figure "allows one to express one's almost religious feeling about life," and he confirmed this by painting two excellent portraits of his wife that same year — *Woman with a Hat* and *Madame Matisse: "The Green Line"* (Plate 31).

The Full Maturity of Fauvism

Woman with a Hat, along with other paintings done in Collioure, formed part of the historic Salon d'Automne of 1905 that shocked the Parisians of the time, but it later became the symbol of the Fauvist movement. In spite of adverse criticism, however, the Fauves slowly began, even at that time, to be accepted by many. Some of the least conservative and imaginative collectors and art dealers became interested in the Fauves and were able to sell their works by virtue of the controversy created around the group.

Vlaminck

Among some of the more fortunate artists who succeeded in selling their works without difficulty were Matisse, Derain, and Vlaminck, to whom Vollard had given a contract. Vlaminck's paintings of 1906 were perhaps the best of his entire artistic career since they faithfully mirrored all that he had discovered and learned in the past few years, but they were also new in their exceptional chromatic variations. From the firm and simplified structure of *Landscape with Red*

Trees (Plate 33) and the agile line of *Carrières-sur-Seine* (Plate 32) to the sensuous opulence of his *The Tugboat* (Plate 34), we find nothing but a progressive, almost dizzy, conquest of color.

For many of the Fauvists the movement may have been only an adolescent adventure or a stepping-stone to greater artistic endeavors, but for Vlaminck it was undoubtedly the instrument that allowed him to express himself in the most complete manner. That may explain why, after the Fauvist painters went their separate ways and new styles became popular, in the eyes of some critics, Vlaminck's paintings never again succeeded in achieving the extraordinary quality that distinguished his art in 1906.

Matisse

Matisse, who in the spring of 1906 exhibited *The Joy of Life* at the Salon des Indépendants, remained the leader of the group through his series of important works that included landscapes, portraits, and still lifes. While in his beautiful *The Gypsy* (Plate 37) the bright tones are an outstanding feature, his *Self-Portrait* in Copenhagen achieves its dramatic intensity with somber undertones. The range of this work demonstrates clearly Matisse's absolute freedom of style — a style that continued to grow and to change, a style that was not conditioned by any specific formula. We also find great variety in his still lifes — from the one with the "pink onion" to his famous *Still Life with Red Carpet* (Plate 36), which lends extraordinary lyricism to an otherwise purely decorative theme.

Derain

The year 1906 was also an extremely happy one for Derain. He returned to London, where he had been at the end of 1905. In Derain's London paintings we see new themes and new lights that suggest cold, delicate tones in his landscapes as he practiced the Fauvist theories in an atmosphere far away from the Mediterranean. Some of his views of London, the Thames, and Westminster Bridge, with translucent colors vaguely reminiscent of the English landscapist Turner, rank among Derain's most beautiful canvases.

Dufy and Marquet

Raoul Dufy and Albert Marquet in the meantime drew closer to each other, both in their art and in their personal lives. They spent some time together first at Fécamp, Honfleur, and Le Havre on the English Channel, then at Trouville and Cannes in the south of France working under the bright Mediterranean sun. The Trouville posters, the fourteenth of July celebrations in Saint-Tropez, and the port and the beach in Le Havre were some of the themes that inspired them and that they depicted with striking originality. It is of interest to note, during this period, the great similarity in their artistic expression. Perhaps the only thing that distinguishes their work is the fact that Dufy prefers loud colors and delights in precision and detail while Marquet, who only rarely brightens his canvas with a colorful brushstroke (the red flag and the blue collars of sailors in *The Beach at Fécamp* (Plate 49), usually maintains a more harmonious and narrower chromatic gamut (*Fair at Le Havre,* Plate 45).

Braque and Friesz

The year 1906 was also the year in which Georges Braque completely embraced Fauvism. Although he maintained a friendly rapport with Dufy and Friesz in Paris, he did not become close to Matisse until 1907—at the time when Fauvism had already begun to disappear as a coherent movement.

Braque's father and uncle were both amateur painters, and he grew up in an atmosphere in which the Impressionist painters were still highly admired; therefore he had a difficult time in liberating himself from their tradition. However, Braque assiduously tried to free himself from the Impressionist influence and from a style that he considered to have served its purpose already. At the Salon d'Automne of 1905 Braque was first drawn to the Fauves' use of color, and here he found a new freedom of artistic idiom. His Fauvist paintings date from 1906 to the spring of 1907 and total about forty.

Braque's first Fauvist paintings were done in Antwerp, where he visited with Friesz. Both were inspired by the active life of the port—the comings and goings of ships, the flying banners, and the changing reflections on the tranquil waters. Their styles are very similar—much more sober than the rest of the Fauves—and yellow-oranges amid green and red brushstrokes appear frequently in their works. But while it is difficult to see a preconceived order in Friesz's paintings, Braque organized his compositions with a kind of elegance and sobriety that distinguish him from the rest of the Fauves. Even more original were his later structured and refined landscapes of Estaque. At times Braque adopted the Pointillist technique but with extreme temperance, using few colors and many luminous effects as in *Cove at La Ciotat* (Plate 54). Perhaps Othon Friesz's best painting was done in 1907, *Portrait of the Poet Fernand Fleuret* (Plate 55). This portrait places the intense, expressive young poet in the midst of the bright chromatic contrasts reminiscent of Matisse's first interiors.

Van Dongen

Somehow separate from the rest of the Fauves, although he exhibited his works with them, Kees van Dongen achieved a style that is actually closer to Expressionism. His Fauvist paintings between 1905 and 1907 were of a very personal nature. Sometimes his sensitivity with regard to decorative effects is worthy of Matisse, and sometimes his vibrant chromatic explosions are reminiscent of Vlaminck's work. And yet he is substantially different from both artists. In fact, Van Dongen used the Fauvist language to express the fascinating, ephemeral images that he saw in the picturesque world of circuses and cabarets of the vanishing era of *La Bohème*. His talent as a portrait painter and his predilection for feminine figures allowed him a financially successful career. However, this same facile talent also conditioned his style and divested his work of the unforgettable zeal found in so many of the paintings he completed during his Fauvist period.

In 1906 all the Fauves showed their works at the now traditional Salon d'Automne. After all the years of growth and a brief time of maturity, the movement had reached its peak and was by then in its decline. The following year brought other interests on the artistic scene, and there were significant currents in the air that soon were to announce a new revolution. While Matisse continued along the same lines, all the others were influenced by the more progressive trends and styles.

It was at this time—in 1906—that Picasso was working on his *Demoiselles d'Avignon* in his atelier in Bateau Lavoir and was preparing the foundations for Cubism, the next and last of the twentieth-century revolutions. Braque was in contact with Picasso, and in La Ciotat and in L'Estaque he experimented with a constructive use of color leaning toward an organized synthesis instead of the frenetic, chromatic explosion of the recent past. Derain too took a similar road away from Fauvism and followed in Cézanne's footsteps.

By 1907, when the Salon d'Automne gave a retrospective exhibition of Cézanne and Van Gogh, the great masters from Aix, it was obvious that the avant-garde was beginning to find new directions. Cézanne's art, so opportunely revived in that moment of transition, was the determining factor in the evolution of painting as Van Gogh and Gauguin's retrospective exhibitions had been for the Fauves.

Fauvism as a movement lasted until 1907. It was, one might say, a fever, a youthful dream that existed only about three years. In spite of these characteristics, which lead many to think of it as a parenthesis in the history of art, Fauvism is really of great and lasting importance. Its healthy reaction against the conventionality of the nineteenth century served as a means of achieving the freedom of expression that laid the groundwork for modern art. The works of Matisse, Braque, and Derain have almost inevitably influenced — and often inspired — the painters of our time.

If today — after more than half a century and after all the evolution and revolutions that have modified man's world and consequently the world of art — Fauvism appears as an episode that occurred long ago, we must not forget that Fauvism served a stimulating and productive function for the twentieth century. From the German Expressionists to Chagall, from Kandinsky to Soutine, and in certain abstract currents since World War II, all those who have believed in exploring the many possible uses of color are in some way deeply indebted to the Fauves.

PLATES

The Beginnings of Fauvism

PLATE 1   HENRI MATISSE *Toulouse Landscape,* 1898–99 (40 x 29 cm) Paris, Georges Renand
Collection

PLATE 2   HENRI MATISSE *The Invalid,* 1899 (46 x 38 cm) Baltimore, Museum of Art, Cone Collection

PLATE 3   HENRI MATISSE *Interior with Harmonium,* 1900 (75 x 55 cm) Nice, Musée Matisse

PLATE 4   ALBERT MARQUET *Life Class at the École des Beaux-Arts,* 1898 (73 x 50 cm) Bordeaux,
Musée des Beaux-Arts

PLATE 5   ALBERT MARQUET *Notre Dame,* 1904 (73 x 60 cm) Pau, Musée des Beaux-Arts

PLATE 6 HENRI MATISSE *The Terrace of Paul Signac at Saint-Tropez*, 1904 (72 x 58 cm) Boston, Isabella Stewart Gardner Museum

PLATE 7   HENRI MATISSE *Luxe, calme et volupté,* 1904–1905 (95 x 116 cm) Paris, Private Collection (Photo: Mercurio)

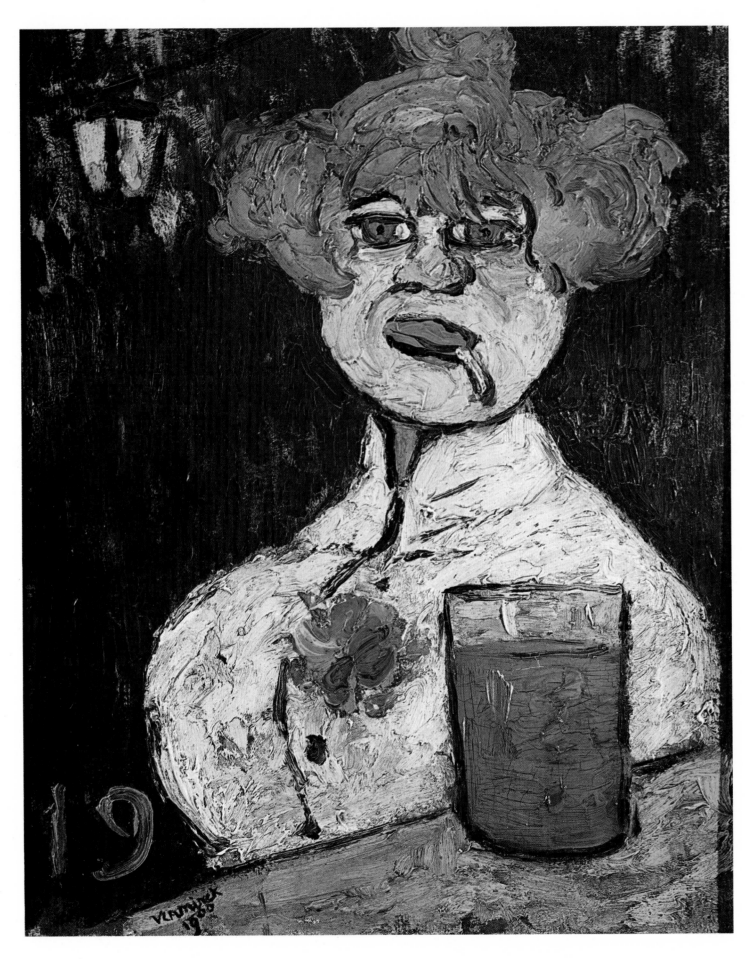

PLATE 8   MAURICE VLAMINCK *At the Bar*, 1900 (40 x 32 cm) Avignon, Musée Calvet

PLATE 9   MAURICE VLAMINCK *The Pond at Saint-Cucufa,* 1903 (54 x 65 cm) Paris, B. Fize Collection

PLATE 10 MAURICE VLAMINCK *Kitchen Interior,* 1904 (56 x 45 cm) Paris, Musée National d'Art Moderne

PLATE 11   MAURICE VLAMINCK *Houses at Chatou,* 1903 (82.5 x 100 cm) Chicago, Art Institute of Chicago (Gift of Mr. and Mrs. Maurice E. Culberg)

PLATE 12   ANDRÉ DERAIN *Barges,* 1904 (79 x 97 cm) Paris, B. Fize Collection

PLATE 13   ANDRÉ DERAIN *The Old Tree*, 1904–1905 (41 x 33 cm) Paris, Musée National d'Art Moderne

Around the Protagonists

PLATE 14   Louis Valtat *The Madeleine-Bastille Omnibus, c.* 1895 (130 x 152 cm) Geneva, Musée Petit Palais

PLATE 15   Louis Valtat *The Seine and the Eiffel Tower*, 1904 (45 x 60 cm) Paris, B. Fize Collection

PLATE 16   Jean Puy *Landscape*, 1904 (73 x 92 cm) Paris, Musée National d'Art Moderne

PLATE 17   CHARLES CAMOIN *Portrait of Albert Marquet, c.* 1904 (92 x 73 cm) Paris, Musée National d'Art
Moderne

PLATE 18 HENRI MANGUIN *Woman at the Window, Rue Boursault,* 1904 (61 x 50 cm) Paris, Private Collection
(Photo: Mercurio)

PLATE 19   CHARLES CAMOIN *The Negress*, Le Havre, Musée

PLATE 20   HENRI MANGUIN *July 14: Port of Saint-Tropez,* 1905 (61 x 50 cm) Paris, Lucile Manguin Collection

PLATE 21   CHARLES CAMOIN *The Port of Marseilles,* 1904 (65 x 81 cm) Le Havre, Musée

PLATE 22   ALBERT MARQUET *The Port of Saint-Tropez*, 1905 (65 x 81 cm) Saint-Tropez, Musée de l'Annonciade

PLATE 23 RAOUL DUFY *On the Beach at Saint-Adresse*, 1904 (66 x 82 cm) Rouen, Musée des Beaux-Arts

PLATE 24   RAOUL DUFY *Old Houses on the Harbor of Honfleur,* 1906 (60 x 73 cm) Paris, formerly in the collection of Dr. A. Roudinesco

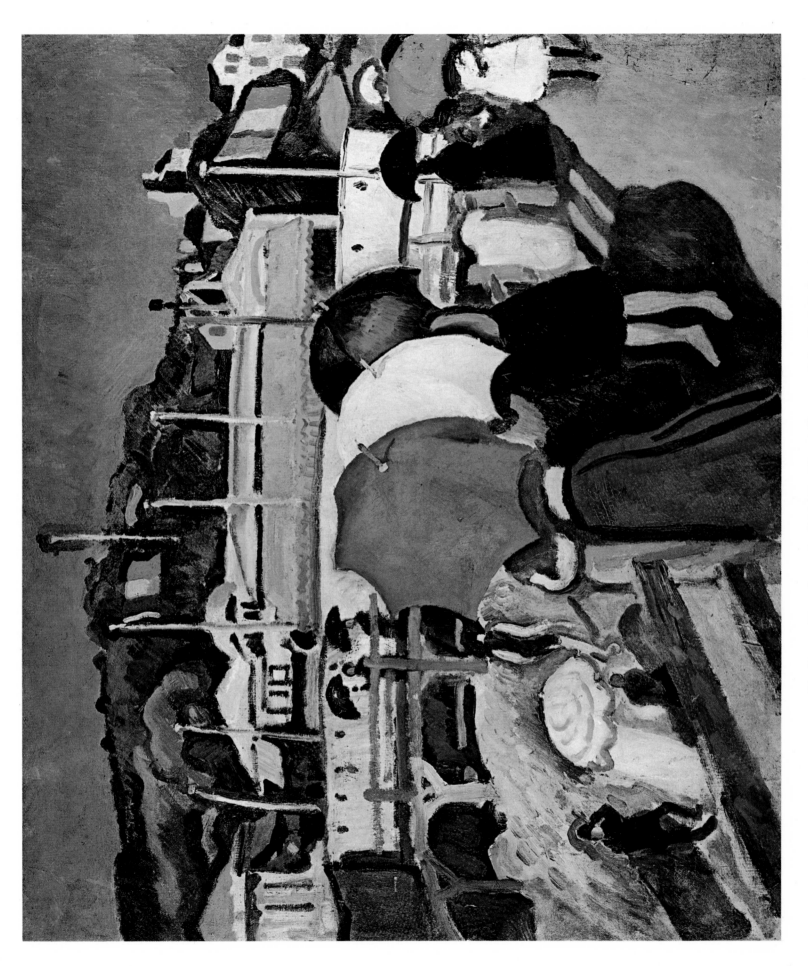

PLATE 25　Raoul Dufy *Parasols*, 1906 (60 x 73 cm) Houston, John Beck Collection

PLATE 26   ALBERT MARQUET *View of Agay,* 1905 (65 x 80 cm) Paris, Musée National d'Art Moderne

44

Matisse and Derain at Collioure

PLATE 27   HENRI MATISSE *Pastoral,* 1905 (46 x 55 cm) Paris, Musée National d'Art Moderne

PLATE 28 Henri Matisse *Interior at Collioure*, 1905 (60 x 73 cm) Zurich, Private Collection

PLATE 29 ANDRÉ DERAIN *Portrait of Henri Matisse*, 1905 (33 x 40.5 cm) Philadelphia, Museum of Art, A. E. Gallatin Collection

PLATE 30   HENRI MATISSE *Study for "The Joy of Life,"* 1905 (46.5 x 53 cm) Copenhagen, Statens Museum for Kunst

PLATE 31   HENRI MATISSE *Madame Matisse: "The Green Line,"* 1905 (40 x 32 cm) Copenhagen, Statens Museum for Kunst

Vlaminck

PLATE 32   MAURICE VLAMINCK *Carrières-sur-Seine*, 1906 (54 x 65 cm) Paris, Private Collection

PLATE 33   MAURICE VLAMINCK *Landscape with Red Trees,* 1906 (54 x 65 cm) Paris, Musée National d'Art Moderne

PLATE 34   MAURICE VLAMINCK *The Tugboat*, 1905 (58.5 x 73.5 cm) New York, Mrs. Samuel Weiner Collection

PLATE 35 MAURICE VLAMINCK *Portrait of a Woman,* 1906 (73 x 60 cm) Zurich, Dr. Milton Guggenheim Collection

Matisse

PLATE 37   HENRI MATISSE *The Gypsy*, 1905–1906 (55 x 46 cm) Saint-Tropez, Musée de l'Annonciade

PLATE 38   HENRI MATISSE *Young Sailor* (Version II), 1906 (100 x 78 cm) Chicago, Mr. and Mrs. Leigh B. Block Collection

PLATE 39 HENRI MATISSE *Marguerite Reading,* 1906 (65 x 80 cm) Grenoble, Musée de Peinture et de Sculpture

Derain

PLATE 40   ANDRÉ DERAIN *Reflections on the Water,* 1905 (81 x 100 cm) Saint-Tropez, Musée de l'Annonciade

PLATE 41 ANDRÉ DERAIN *Bridge on the Thames*, 1906 (80 x 99 cm) Saint-Tropez, Musée de l'Annonciade

PLATE 42   ANDRÉ DERAIN *Westminster Bridge*, 1906 (80 x 100 cm) Paris, Private Collection

PLATE 43   ANDRÉ DERAIN *Three Figures Seated on the Grass*, 1906–1907 (38 x 55 cm) Paris, Musée National d'Art Moderne

Marquet and Dufy

PLATE 44   RAOUL DUFY *Port of Le Havre,* 1906 (60 x 73 cm) Nantes, Musée des Beaux-Arts

PLATE 45   Albert Marquet *Fair at Le Havre,* 1906 (65 x 81 cm) Bordeaux, Musée des Beaux-Arts

PLATE 46   ALBERT MARQUET *Fourteenth of July,* 1906 (79 x 63 cm) Paris, Private Collection

PLATE 47   RAOUL DUFY *Street Decked with Flags,* 1906 (81 x 65 cm) Paris, Musée National d'Art Moderne

PLATE 48   RAOUL DUFY *Billboards at Trouville,* 1906 (65 x 88 cm) Paris, Musée National d'Art Moderne

PLATE 49   ALBERT MARQUET *The Beach at Fécamp*, 1906 (50 x 61 cm) Paris, Musée National d'Art Moderne

Braque and Friesz

PLATE 50   GEORGES BRAQUE *Harbor of Antwerp*, 1905 (50.5 x 61.5 cm) Basel, Kunstmuseum (Gift of E. Hoffman)

PLATE 51   OTHON FRIESZ *Harbor of Antwerp*, 1906 (60.5 x 73 cm) Paris, Robert Lebel Collection

PLATE 52 GEORGES BRAQUE *The Yellow Seacoast or Boats in the Bay*, 1906 (50 x 70 cm) Los Angeles, County Museum of Art

PLATE 53   GEORGES BRAQUE *View of L'Estaque,* 1906 (60 x 73 cm) Saint-Tropez, Musée de l'Annonciade

PLATE 54   GEORGES BRAQUE *Cove at La Ciotat*, 1907 (36 x 48 cm) Paris, Musée National d'Art Moderne

PLATE 55   OTHON FRIESZ *Portrait of the Poet Fernand Fleuret,* 1907, (76 x 60 cm) Paris, Musée National d'Art
Moderne

Van Dongen

PLATE 56   KEES VAN DONGEN *Woman of Montmartre*, 1930, Le Havre, Musée

PLATE 57 KEES VAN DONGEN *The Red Clown,* 1905 (74 x 60 cm) Paris, Lucile Manguin Collection

PLATE 58   KEES VAN DONGEN *Femme fatale*, 1905 (80 x 60 cm) Paris, Private Collection

PLATE 59   KEES VAN DONGEN *Fatima and Her Troupe,* 1906 (100 x 81 cm) Paris, B. Fize Collection

PLATE 60   KEES VAN DONGEN *Woman at the Balustrade*, 1907–1910 (80 x 99 cm) Saint-Tropez, Musée de l'Annonciade

THE ARTISTS

GEORGES BRAQUE

Born in the French town of Argenteuil-sur-Seine on May 13, 1882. Eight years later his family moved to Le Havre, where Braque went to school and, as a young man, attended courses at an art school along with Othon Friesz and Raoul Dufy. Braque's love for painting grew under the guidance of his teacher Lhullier, and in 1900 he went to Paris to devote himself exclusively to the study of art. In Paris he attended the Humbert Academy and then

the Beaux-Arts School, where he managed to break away from the Impressionist influence that had been so important in his early years. The use of color as practiced by the Fauves helped him achieve this and provided him with a model of free expression upon which he developed his style. Braque joined the Fauves in 1906 and remained associated with them until 1907. He worked closely with Friesz, and exhibited his works at the salons between 1906 and 1907 with the rest of the Fauves. The art dealer Kahnweiler gave Braque a contract and introduced him to Apollinaire, who brought him into contact with Picasso. In the years that followed, Picasso and Braque became the leading Cubist painters. They spent the summer of 1911 together at Céret and that of 1912 at Sorgues, where Braque returned after being invalided out of the French Army in World War I. Braque served with distinction and was seriously wounded. He took up painting once more after his discharge in 1916 and in 1920 re-established his friendship with

Kahnweiler. By then Braque's art had achieved full maturity, and he was widely recognized. He lived in Paris, but in 1930 he built a country home near Dieppe. In 1945 he was stricken by a serious illness that forced him to remain inactive for a long period of time. When he started painting once again, he became world famous through a retrospective exhibit of his works in 1947 and by a prize given to him by the Venice Biennale in 1948. Braque died in Paris on August 31, 1963.

CHARLES CAMOIN

Born in Marseilles on September 23, 1879. He was introduced to painting at an early age by his parents, who were professional decorators. In Marseilles he attended the fine arts school, and later moved to Paris, where he enrolled at the Moreau atelier. There he met Matisse and Manguin. He met Cézanne in 1902 during his military service at Aix-en-Provence. This meeting left a profound impression on Camoin and strongly influenced his art. After his military service he started a long correspondence with Cézanne that continued un-

BRAQUE *Harbor of Antwerp, Mainmast,* 1906, Solingen-Ohligs, B. Glauerdt Collection

CAMOIN *Rue Bouterie,* 1904, Paris, Private Collection

til the latter's death. Camoin exhibited his works for the first time at the Salon des Indépendants in 1903 along with Matisse, Manguin, and other Fauves. His art, which was less revolutionary and aggressive than his colleagues', met with a certain success, and some of the leading dealers began to buy his paintings. Camoin spent his summers on the Côte d'Azur and was so taken by the Mediterranean seacoast that he bought a house in Saint-Tropez. Even in his Fauve period, instead of showing the chromatic violence that was so typical of this movement, he showed a predilection for luminous effects and delicate subjects such as flowers, landscapes, and the female figure. Camoin slowly moved away from Fauvism and even repudiated some of his earlier Fauvist works. He spent the rest of his life between Paris and Saint-Tropez. He died in Paris on May 20, 1965.

VLAMINCK *Portrait of André Derain*

DERAIN *Banks of the Seine*, 1904, Paris, Musée National d'Art Moderne

ANDRÉ DERAIN

Born June 7, 1880, in Chatou, France. He went to school at Le Vesinet and then in Paris. He decided to become an artist against the will of his father, who wanted him to be an engineer. Between 1898 and 1899 Derain attended the Carrière Academy, where he met Matisse. During this period he became acquainted with the works of the Impressionists, with Cézanne, Gauguin, and with the classical masters on display at the Louvre. In 1900 he met Vlaminck, who became a great source of intellec-

tual inspiration for him. Between 1901 and 1904 he completed his military service and prepared the illustrations for two of Vlaminck's novels. By this time he had become reconciled with his family and had enrolled in the Académie Julian. In 1905 he was able to sell some of his paintings. That summer he went to Collioure (Pyrenees) with Matisse and later on had an exhibition of his works at the Salon d'Automne. Derain then spent some time in London, where he painted the Thames and its bridges. He met Picasso in Paris, and in 1908 spent some time with him in Avignon. At that point Derain ended his Fauvist period and turned toward a new interpretation of form based on the teachings of Cézanne. In 1910 he went again to Spain with Picasso and became interested in Cubism but never fully accepted it. In the years after World War I, Derain's art became more and more realistic. In 1921 he went to Italy and studied the art from Pompeii. Upon returning to France he dedicated himself to portrait painting and received great critical acclaim. Nonetheless, he was accused of betraying modern painting for the sake of tradition. In 1935 he moved to Chambourcy and continued painting until his death on September 8, 1954.

RAOUL DUFY

Born in Le Havre on June 3, 1877. He began working at the age of fourteen and went to evening school at the municipal school in Le Havre, where he took art lessons. His classmates were Othon Friesz and Georges Braque. In 1899 he was given a scholarship to the Ecole des Beaux-Arts in Paris, where, along with Friesz, he was a frequent visitor to Leon Bonnat's studio. In 1901 Dufy exhibited his paintings at the Salon des Artistes Français, in 1903 at the Salon des Indépendants, and in 1905 at the Salon d'Automne. He had his first one-man show at the Berthe Weill Gallery in 1906. From 1904 on Dufy was in contact with the Fauves and was highly influenced by Matisse. The years 1907 and 1908 were years of strong Cubist influence during which Dufy's canvases became severe and almost monochromatic. He also designed textiles for Poiret and did a series of drawings for Apollinaire's *Bestiaïre*. He joined the army in 1914 and served throughout the war. In 1920 Dufy settled in Vence

Dufy *Beach at Saint-Adresse*, 1904, Paris, Musée National d'Art Moderne

scenery for the ballet *Palm Beach*. Dufy also did a number of book illustrations, and in 1937 he designed a large panel entitled *Electricity* for the Universal Exhibit in Paris. He traveled widely in France and finally, suffering from arthritis, settled in Perpignon. In 1947 he had a large one-man show at the Louis Carré Gallery in Paris. In 1950 he went to the United States and had two one-man shows in New York. He was awarded the International Prize for Painting at the Venice Bienniale in 1952. Raoul Dufy died on March 23, 1953, at Forcalquier in Provence.

OTHON FRIESZ

Born in 1879 in Le Havre, where he spent his childhood. Along with his adventurous spirit and his love for the sea, which was so characteristic of the Fauves, he developed a passion for painting, which he studied along with Braque

Friesz *La Ciotat*, 1905, Paris, Musée National d'Art Moderne

Photograph of Raoul Dufy in his studio

on the Mediterranean, where he painted a number of landscapes and also worked with ceramics and wood engraving. In 1922 he went to Taormina with his friend Pierre Courthion, and in 1926 he visited Morocco with Poiret. Following these trips his landscapes took on a new note of luminosity. In 1925 he took part in the International Exhibit of Decorative Arts in Paris. In 1930 he designed the

83

and Dury under the teacher Lhullier. In 1897 he decided to dedicate himself to painting despite his parents' objections, and he moved to Paris. There Friesz met Bonnat, who welcomed him to his atelier in spite of the fact that he did not agree with the Impressionist bent of his young student's canvases. Friesz spent some carefree years and was a notorious bohemian. However, in his art he sought to develop a style that would free him from the influence of Impressionism. In doing so he carefully studied Matisse's work. Friesz became an associate of Matisse in 1905, and in that year became one of the Fauves. He went to Antwerp with Braque and together they painted the river and the port in an almost identical style. The two also went to Estaque and La Ciotat, where Friesz gradually turned to Cézanne's paintings for inspiration. In the meantime, his paintings had achieved relative success. In 1907 Friesz sold eight of his paintings for 2,000 francs, a fairly high price for the times. From then on he had nothing but success, and this provided him the opportunity to occupy certain institutional posts: after teaching at the Scandinavian Academy, he took the position of principal of a fine arts school. Between 1911 and the start of World War II Friesz made several trips to Belgium, Portugal, Italy, and the United States. He died in Paris on January 10, 1949.

MANGUIN *Nude in the Studio,* 1903, Paris, André Martinais Collection

HENRI MANGUIN

Born in Paris in 1874 into a middle-class family who, rather than discouraging his study of art, gave him considerable moral support throughout his career. In 1895 he joined the Moreau atelier, where he met Matisse, Marquet, Puy, and Camoin. Manguin was an excellent craftsman and was among the first of the artists who were to become the Fauves to develop a style that used pure colors. He continued his friendship with the rest of the Fauves even after Moreau's death, and often met

MANGUIN *Self-Portrait*

with them at his own atelier on the rue Boursault. In 1902 Manguin exhibited his paintings for the first time at the Salon des Indépendents, and in 1904 at the Salon d'Automne. From 1905 on he spent his summers in Saint-Tropez, where he bought a house called "L'Oustalet." During World War I he sought refuge in Switzerland. His favorite themes were landscapes, nudes, and women. After the war he returned to Paris but spent each summer in Saint-Tropez, where he died on September 25, 1949.

ALBERT MARQUET

Born in Bordeaux on March 26, 1875, into a family of modest means. He attended public school in his native city and showed an unusual interest in art at an early age—so much so that his mother decided to move to Paris so that he could have a proper art education. In 1890 he joined the School of Decorative Arts, where he met Henri Matisse and formed a friendship that lasted the rest of his life. Some years later the two joined Gustave Moreau's atelier. During this time, in order to make a living, both Marquet and Matisse took a job with a company that had been commissioned to decorate the Grand Palais for the Universal Exhibit of 1900. Marquet painted wreaths at twenty francs an hour. That same year one of his paintings was shown at the Salon of the National Society, and later his paintings were exhibited at the Salon des Indépendents and at the Berthe Weill Gallery. In 1905 his paintings were hung along with those of Matisse, Derain, and Vlaminck in the famous room of the Salon d'Automne, which inspired Vauxcelles to write the sentence that coined the name Fauve. From 1905 on, Marquet met with relative success. He also began traveling—he went to Saint-Tropez and to Normandy. During these years he was very much part of the Fauves. The critic Natanson described him as a timid and taciturn young man who was nonetheless strong and self-assured. He traveled throughout France and also visited Germany, Italy, Monaco, Morocco, and the Netherlands. In 1923 he married the writer Marcelle Marty and visited Algiers with her. His urge to travel also took him to Egypt, Rumania, the Soviet Union, and the Scandinavian coun-

MARQUET *Nude*, 1898

MARQUET *Self-Portrait*

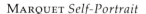

tries. However, he never forgot to paint his beloved Paris. He took refuge in Algiers during the Nazi occupation of France but returned to Paris in 1945, where he died on June 14, 1947.

HENRI MATISSE

Born in Le Cateau in the north of France, on December 31, 1869, into a family of modest means. When he finished secondary school, he studied law to prepare for a job as a civil servant. Unlike so many artists, Matisse apparently had no early interest in painting. His interest in art was awakened during a long hospital stay in 1891 when his mother took Matisse a box of paints to distract him. Henri started to paint and the so-called distraction became so important that, in spite of his father's opposition, he left for Paris some time later in order to learn how to paint. It was very

MATISSE *Self-Portrait*, 1941

vacation at Belle-Île, he met the sculptor Rodin. Under Rodin's direction Matisse began a serious study of sculpture. Between 1901 and 1904 he had grave economic difficulties, and his wife had to work as a milliner to help make ends meet. Finally, from 1904 on, things began looking better: his paintings started to sell. Soon art collectors sought him out and he became internationally famous. In the meantime Matisse continued to exhibit his paintings not only at private shows but also at the Salon d'Automne during his leadership of the Fauvist movement. In 1908 he opened his own academy, and the following year he made his home at Issy-les-Moulineaux. Even after several trips abroad (Algiers, Italy, Germany, Spain, Russia, and Morocco), he was still most inspired by the Mediterranean landscape. In 1921 Matisse settled on the Côte d'Azur, where he spent many peaceful years amid ever-growing fame. He died at Cimiez on November 3, 1954. He was buried there in the splendid Mediterranean light that had nourished his inimitable vision.

difficult for him in the beginning. He lived in poverty and studied in the studio of the leading Academician Bouguereau, but without a great deal of enthusiasm. From 1892 on, he attended the evening classes at the School of Decorative Arts, and finally in 1895 joined the Moreau atelier at the insistence of Moreau himself, who had come to appreciate his work. During a summer

JEAN PUY

Born in Roanne in Provence on November 8, 1876, into a long-established and fairly well-to-do middle-class family. After attending the Ecole des Beaux-Arts in Lyon, he went to Paris and enrolled at the Académie Julian and later attended Carrière's lectures. He met Matisse and Derain and was strongly influenced by them. In 1901 he exhibited his works at the Salon des Indépendents and thereafter continued showing with the Fauves. As in Camoin's case, he too found it easy to sell his works. Puy worked alone and quietly, finding inspiration both in the Brittany countryside and in the feminine figure. He died in Roanne in 1960. Three years later the Lyon Museum had a retrospective exhibit of his work, which rendered homage to his long and passionate artistic career.

MATISSE *Woman with the Hat*, 1905, San Francisco, Walter A. Haas Collection

LOUIS VALTAT

Born in Dieppe, Normandy, on August 8, 1869. He spent his childhood in Versailles, where his family moved soon after his birth. His father was a shipowner but enjoyed painting as a hobby and never opposed Louis' artistic interest. Valtat joined the Académie Julian in 1888 and there became close to the Nabis group, particularly with

Bonnard and Vuillard, who influenced his painting significantly. His friendship with the Pointillist painters was a strong influence in his formative years. His luminous canvases of 1895–1896 are considered precursors of Fauvist art. He was married in 1899 and lived briefly at Antheor in a little house on the beach, which was a great source of inspiration for him. In 1900 the dealer Vollard, who believed in Valtat's work, gave him an exclusive contract. In 1905, five of his paintings were shown at the historic Salon d'Automne. After World War I he settled in Paris but traveled often to Brittany, Normandy, and Chevreuse. He died in Paris in 1952 after four years of blindness.

KEES VAN DONGEN

Born in the Netherlands near Rotterdam, on January 26, 1877, and destined to be one of the most notorious Parisian painters, as well as the most sophisticated of the Fauves. His father was in the beer business. At the age of twelve, young Kees, who had already become interested in painting, was expelled from school, and his parents sent him to the School of Decorative Arts. At the age of eighteen he ran away from home and made his way to New York as a stowaway on a ship. However, he was disappointed by this experience and returned to Rotterdam, where he worked as an illustrator on a newspaper. Two years later he left for Paris determined to become an artist. He held numerous menial jobs

in order to survive but took it all in such good spirits that he soon became one of the most picturesque characters of the bohemian life. He did not make progress in his painting, however, and because of this, as well as for economic reasons, he returned to his country a year later. There he became an illustrator once more in order to make enough money to be able to return to Paris. He did return in 1900 but life, just as diffi-

Matisse *Seated Woman, c.* 1906

cult as before, became even more complicated with his marriage and the birth of a daughter. He settled in Bateau Lavoir and there became friends with Picasso, with whom he sold his canvases on the streets for twenty francs. In 1904 a critic, Fénéon, persuaded the dealer Vollard to give van

VALTAT *The Merry-Go-Round*, 1895–96, Paris, Musée National d'Art Moderne

Dongen a one-man show, which awakened the interest of some critics. His paintings were also shown at the Salon des Indépendents and in 1905 at the Salon d'Automne with the rest of the Fauves. This was his best artistic period. In 1907 the art dealer Kahnweiler gave him a good contract, and the Bernheim brothers surpassed this the following year. The time of famine was over for van Dongen. He settled down in comfortable surroundings, made long trips, and became prominent in Parisian society. His ties with Countess Cassati, a most beautiful and fascinating protagonist of aristocratic French life, gained him entry into the most exclusive Parisian circles. Van Dongen lived in luxurious hotels in Cannes and Deauville, where he frequented the casinos and horse races along with rich and fashionable Parisians. He painted a series of portraits as frivolous and fascinating as the women he seduced. His paintings were, however, a chronicle of a society that was to collapse during the Great Depression of the 1930s. After World War II, van

Dongen abandoned his luxurious Parisian homes and retired to the Côte d'Azur with his second wife, Marie-Claire. He died there in 1968 at the age of ninety-one.

MAURICE DE VLAMINCK

Born in Paris on April 4, 1876, into a family of music instructors who came originally from Flanders. He was the wildest of all the wild beasts among the artists of the movement called Fauvism. He was raised in the country in Le Vesinet, and at sixteen years of age left his family and settled in Chatou. After working as a mechanic for some time, he earned his living as a professional bicycle racer. At eighteen he was already married and had a daughter, Madeleine. Besides bicycle racing, he turned to music and supported his family by giving violin lessons and playing in small orchestras on Sunday. Vlaminck was always a restless soul and became politically involved in anarchism. Finally he found expression for his restlessness in painting and writing. From childhood he had shown a flair for painting,

Photograph of Kees van Dongen in his studio, 1909

VAN DONGEN *One-eyed Dancer Bowing*, 1905–1906, Paris, Private Collection

his successes multiplied, he isolated himself more and more, finding refuge only in writing and painting. In 1956 the Charpentier Gallery celebrated his eightieth year with a retrospective exhibit of his work. Two years later Vlaminck died in his country house at Tourillière.

but it was only after his meeting with Derain that art became the determining interest and drive in his life. Vlaminck shied away from academic painting and expressed in his art his violent and unconventional view of nature. Van Gogh influenced him deeply, and Matisse, whom he met in Paris, left a subtle but positive imprint on his art. Vlaminck showed his paintings with the Fauves in 1904, and in 1905 eight of his paintings were hung at the Salon d'Automne. Vollard gave him a contract that permitted him to dedicate himself exclusively to art and to participate in the polemics of the avant-garde. He was part of the Cubist movement in its early years, but soon abandoned it in favor of a style strongly influenced by Cézanne. He went to war in 1914 and returned tormented by a deep moral crisis. At this time Vlaminck had become well known and apparently was able to lead a more peaceful life, but in reality he found no peace. His autobiography, *Tournant dangereux*, bears witness to his internal conflicts. Not even age brought him peace, and while

VLAMINCK *Self-Portrait*

List of Illustrations

Translated by Himilce Novas

Permission by A.D.A.G.P. by French Reproduction Rights 1970, for the works of Georges Braque, Charles Camoin, André Derain, Othon Friesz, Henri Manguin, Jean Puy, Albert Marquet

Permission by S.P.A.D.E.M. by French Reproduction Rights 1970, for the works of Raoul Dufy, Henri Matisse, Kees van Dongen, Maurice Vlaminck

Printed in Italy by A. Mondadori - Verona